IN AND OUT

AMY CULLIFORD

A Crabtree Roots Book

CRABTREE
Publishing Company
www.crabtreebooks.com

School-to-Home Support for Caregivers and Teachers

This book helps children grow by letting them practice reading. Here are a few guiding questions to help the reader with building his or her comprehension skills. Possible answers appear here in red.

Before Reading:

• What do I think this book is about?
  • *I think this book is about directions.*
  • *I think this book is about things that are inside and things that are outside.*

• What do I want to learn about this topic?
  • *I want to learn what in and out look like.*
  • *I want to learn the difference between in and out.*

During Reading:

• I wonder why...
  • *I wonder why some fish jump out of water.*
  • *I wonder why books are carried in a backpack.*

• What have I learned so far?
  • *I have learned what in and out look like.*
  • *I have learned that some fish can jump out of water.*

After Reading:

• What details did I learn about this topic?
  • *I have learned that it is easier to carry school supplies in a backpack.*
  • *I have learned that apples are sometimes collected in a basket.*

• Read the book again and look for the vocabulary words.
  • *I see the word **apples** on page 3 and the word **fish** on page 7. The other vocabulary words are found on page 14.*

These **apples** are
in a **basket**.

This apple is out.

This **fish** is in the water.

This fish jumps out!

This **book** is in a **backpack**.

This book is out.

Word List

Sight Words

a	is	the
are	jumps	these
in	out	this

Words to Know

apples

backpack

basket

book

fish

30 Words

These **apples** are in a **basket**.

This apple is out.

This **fish** is in the water.

This fish jumps out!

This **book** is in a **backpack**.

This book is out.

Written by: Amy Culliford

Designed by: Rhea Wallace

Series Development: James Earley

Proofreader: Janine Deschenes

Educational Consultant: Marie Lemke M.Ed.

Photographs:
Shutterstock: r.classen: cover, p.1; Photoexpert: p. 3, 14;
   Syzman Kaczarczyk: p. 4-5; Rocksweeper; p. 6, 14;
   costas and dumitrescu: p. 9; ESBProfessional: p. 11, 14;
   wavebreakmedia: p. 13

Library and Archives Canada Cataloguing in Publication

CIP available at Library and Archives Canada

Library of Congress Cataloging-in-Publication Data

CIP available at Library of Congress

Crabtree Publishing Company

www.crabtreebooks.com   1-800-387-7650

Copyright © 2022 **CRABTREE PUBLISHING COMPANY**   Printed in the U.S.A./CG20210915/012022

Published in the United States
Crabtree Publishing
347 Fifth Avenue, Suite 1402-145
New York, NY, 10016

Published in Canada
Crabtree Publishing
616 Welland Ave.
St. Catharines, Ontario L2M 5V6